TRACKERS EARTH GUIDE TO

KNIVES & WOOD CARVING

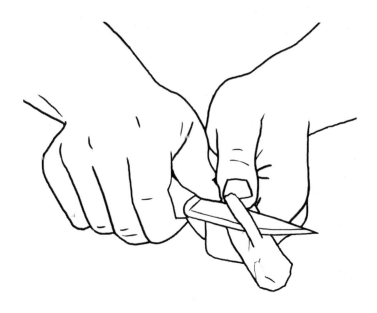

FIRST EDITION

Text & illustration copyright © 2015
by **Trackers Earth Books, LLC**
2nd Printing 2016

All rights reserved. No part of this publication may be reproduced, distributed, or transmitted in any form or by any means, including photocopying, recording, or other electronic or mechanical methods, without the prior written permission of the publisher, except in the case of brief quotations embodied in critical reviews and certain other noncommercial uses permitted by copyright law. For permission requests, write to the publisher, addressed "Attention: Permissions Coordinator," at the address below.

Trackers Earth Books, LLC
4617 Milwaukie Avenue
Portland, OR 97202
(503) 345-3312
www.trackersearth.com

Contributors: Tony Deis and David Jacobson
Editor: Michelle McCann
Designer: Ethan Jewett
Illustrators: Cary Porter, Karen DeWitz and Amelia Davis

A NOTE TO PARENTS & EDUCATORS

This book contains activities that may be dangerous for everyone or may be especially inappropriate for young children. *All of these activities should be carried out under adult supervision.* The authors and publisher expressly disclaim liability for any injury or damages that result from engaging in the activities contained in this book.

Table of Contents

Beginnings

The Time I Almost Cut My Thumb Off   1
How We Begin   3

Principles

8 Blades   8
Wood Secrets   14
Your Knife   19
Carving Stances   25
Carving Grips   29
Carving Secrets   35

Techniques & Projects

Basic Cuts   39
Basic Wood Carving Makes   51
Intermediate Cuts   57
Intermediate Wood Carving Makes   75
Advanced Cuts   81
Advanced Wood Carving Makes   95
Rock Work   103
Sharpening Blades   105
First Aid   119

Beyond Blades

The Rangers Edge   127
Rangers Words   128

1

The Time I Almost Cut My Thumb Off

Once, when I was much younger, I was in the forest throwing knives with friends. I wanted to whip out my blade and launch it at the target in one fluid motion, but I didn't notice that my sheath was splitting apart at the top. The 8-inch razor-sharp knife sliced between my thumb and index finger—only to be stopped by the bone.

I awkwardly sheathed my blade and applied direct pressure to stop the bleeding. I washed the wound as my friend David pulled out the First-aid kit and proceeded to teach himself how to stitch up my cut, all while laughing and making jokes at my expense. For his first time, he did a decent job, but my hand still looked like Frankenstein's monster (see page 119 First Aid for what you *should* do, instead of what I did: seek proper medical care).

The wound healed fine, but to this day I have no feeling at the tip of my left thumb, and it throbs whenever bad weather is coming. Still, it serves as a great reminder to Pay Attention and stay safe with blades. As a kid I learned some lessons the hard way, but even experienced Rangers make mistakes. Hopefully, this book saves you from some of those difficult lessons.

Blades are one of the most useful tools for Forest Craft, whether made of steel, stone, or bone. They can carve, split, and chew away at wood. They help us skin, butcher, and even hunt.

Your blade represents a Ranger's purpose: walking along the edge of the wild, while caring for the Village. Wear it with discipline. Respect it. And keep it sharp.

2

Common sense is no longer common.
—Ranger Tony

How We Begin

Welcome to Trackers Earth. This is where Rangers come to train. The Rangers Guild represents the arts of Forest Craft: wilderness survival, tracking, and stealth. Rangers live by the *Curriculum of Shadows*—a philosophy of invisibility and deep connection to the wild.

The best way to start training is the way we begin everything at Trackers—with three important rules:

Rule No. 1
No One Dies

Rule No. 2
No Wounds That Don't Heal in Four Days

Rule No. 3
Follow the Code of Common Sense

The first two rules are pretty easy to understand, but the third one might need some explaining.

The Code of Common Sense

Our ancestors could light fire, create tools, and build shelter from the land. Those abilities live on within you. Rediscovering them takes time, practice, and patience with yourself—along with the Code of Common Sense:

Rangers Guild
PAY ATTENTION

Push the edges of your awareness: eyes, ears, and all your senses. Keep an open mind and heart. Don't restrict yourself with a narrow view of things. The challenges and opportunities Nature provides often go unseen. Pay Attention to the spaces and places most people ignore.

Wilders Guild
BE TRULY HELPFUL

Understand the difference between what you *believe* is helpful and what is *Truly Helpful*. Complaining about being cold and hungry is not helpful. Building a campfire or catching fish is helpful. When you put the needs of your community first you become Truly Helpful.

Mariners Guild
RESPECT

Many think surviving in nature means struggling against it. Yet, like a Mariner sailing the currents of the sea, we can Flow *with* nature. Take the time to experience the true way of things: creeks, plants, animals, birds, trees, wind, clouds, stars, sun, and moon. By giving your time, appreciation and Respect, you become part of their Flow.

Artisans Guild
YOU'RE DOING IT WRONG, DO IT BETTER

Perfect is boring. There's no perfect way to shoot a bow or weave a basket. There is only progress. Be excited that you're always doing it wrong and there are countless ways to improve. Like the plants, animals and even mountains, you never stop growing. You can always *Do It Better*!

You Are In Charge

The training and missions in this book can be dangerous—the path of a Ranger, even more so. As a Ranger-in-training, you are responsible for yourself.

In this book we give you useful and imperfect advice. Like any good Ranger, we know we're doing it wrong and we must always do it better. You will find many creative challenges we cannot anticipate. It's even possible that you'll get hurt.

Do not do anything that will cause you to break Rule #2, and especially not Rule #1. As a Ranger-in-training, it is up to you to Pay Attention and follow the *Code of Common Sense* to keep you and others safe.

How To Use This Book

Throughout this book you will see three headings: Make, Mission, and Modify. Makes are projects, Missions are tasks, and Modifies are variations on Makes or Missions. All of them will help you learn and practice the skills.

Train Before Trial

An emergency should not be the first time you ever use a blade. Practice your craft well before you need it. As you gain experience you can build upon your training with more advanced skills and challenges.

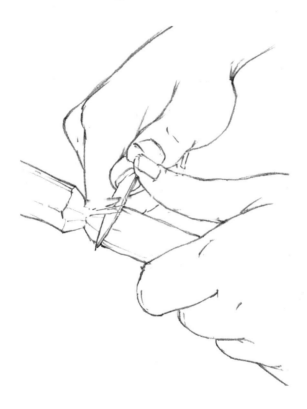

3
The 8 Blades

The 8 Blades are essential principles for working with cutting tools. Like many Rangers Guild skills, the 8 Blades follow the Four Cardinal Directions and the Four Wind Directions.

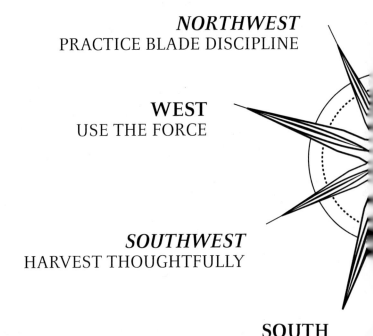

NORTHWEST
PRACTICE BLADE DISCIPLINE

WEST
USE THE FORCE

SOUTHWEST
HARVEST THOUGHTFULLY

SOUTH
GUARD OUTER BLOOD CIRCLE

Honor dictates you place the safety and well-being of others above your own comfort and wants.
—Ranger Chris

NORTH
GUARD INNER BLOOD CIRCLE

NORTHEAST
PROTECT THE VILLAGE

EAST
PAY ATTENTION

SOUTHEAST
STAY SHARP

4 Cardinal Blades: Safety

East Blade
PAY ATTENTION

Stay alert. Injuries happen when you stop Paying Attention. With each cut imagine every potential path your blade could take, and adjust your position to assure complete safety. Don't look away or get distracted; keep your awareness on the cut.

South Blade
GUARD OUTER BLOOD CIRCLE

Imagine a circle as wide as you can reach in every direction with your sheathed blade. Don't let anyone step into your Outer Blood Circle. If they do, stop and sheath your blade if necessary.

West Blade
USE THE FORCE

More force in a cut often leads to less control. The less control, the greater the risk of injury. Consider how much control each technique gives you. As you get better with a blade you achieve a balance—optimizing both control and force.

North Blade
GUARD INNER BLOOD CIRCLE

Your body is filled with blood—don't cause a leak. Imagine any potential path of the blade, keeping your own body, hands, and fingers out of the way of any cut.

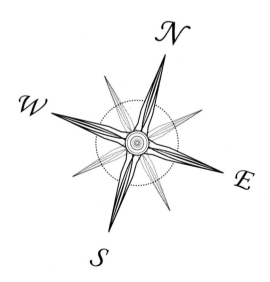

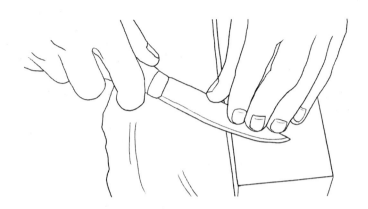

The 4 Wind Blades: Care

Southeast Blade
STAY SHARP

A dull knife is a dangerous knife, requiring more force and potentially causing you to lose control. Maintaining a sharp edge requires less effort than fixing a dull one. A Ranger keeps her blade honed and ready.

Southwest Blade
HARVEST THOUGHTFULLY

Choose wood that closely resembles your finished project. Wood that is straight and free of knots requires less effort to carve. When you cut a living branch or tree, it must have great purpose—caretaking for both Village and forest.

Northwest Blade
PRACTICE BLADE DISCIPLINE

Accept responsibility for your blade. Keep it clean and sheath it when not in use. If you must set down a live (unsheathed) blade, treat it like it could cut at any moment—maintain both Inner and Outer Blood Circles.

Northeast Blade
PROTECT THE VILLAGE

A Ranger protects, caring for the woods, plants, animals, and people of his community (the Village). He does not show off his blade. Today, many see a blade as a frightening weapon instead of a useful tool. Research what type of blade you can have, and leave it at home when required by culture and custom.

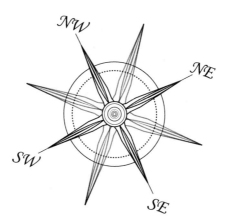

4

Each layer of wood represents a year of a tree's life. With each slice of the blade you erase these moments—all to selfishly make what you want. Remember, take only what you need.
—Old Man Jacobson

Wood Secrets

With the right blade, a Ranger can shape wood into useful tools, containers, and even art. Like your blade, wood must be Respected, not only because carving requires focus, but also because a living tree gives us this gift.

> **RESPECT**
> You might be able to fell a tree quickly, but it takes years for another to grow.

Tiny Branches

Think of one piece of wood like a bunch of very "tiny branches" bundled tightly together. When carving, you first slice through those tiny branches (wood fibers) to peel them away from the rest of the bundle. Slicing through and separating one tiny branch (a thinner layer) can be easier than lifting off two, three, or more (thicker layers).

The Grain

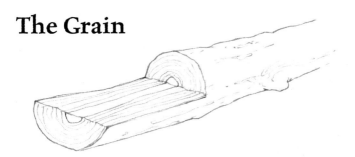

When cutting into wood you see light and dark layers. Every year adds a layer (growth ring) that runs in the same direction the trunk or branch once grew. Cutting *against the grain* of wood can be difficult. Carving or cutting wood is easier when you cut in the same direction the grain runs, or *with the grain.*

PAY ATTENTION
With knots in a stick, the grain changes direction and starts to travel with the branch that created the knot. Because the wood grain "bends" at knots, they are harder to slice through.

Unneeded Bits

Searching for the *right* piece of wood saves you time and effort. It's also safer. When splitting or carving, the straighter the grain and the fewer the knots, the simpler and more effective your carving technique will be. Remember the West Blade: *Use the Force.*

A Ranger understands the principle of Unneeded Bits. She looks for wood shaped like the object she seeks to carve. Need a spoon for your camp kitchen? Take the time to search for the most spoon-shaped piece of wood.

PAY ATTENTION
You can always remove wood, but it's a lot harder to put it back.

MISSION: Carving Sketch

Draw the shape of what you want to carve right onto the wood. In traditional Forest Craft, use charcoal. As you whittle away your lines, draw the object again. These guides are helpful for beginners and for complex projects.

Ask Permission

Trees may not talk like people or walk like animals, but they do live. Each time we take a tree or a branch for carving, we cut away years of growth. While it may seem like a one-way conversation, it never hurts to ask the tree permission before harvesting from it. Building a deep relationship with the plants and animals you depend on for survival makes you a better craftsperson and a more honest Ranger.

Green vs. Seasoned Wood

For Forest Craft, carving softer greenwood (freshly cut) is often easier than carving harder, seasoned wood. When carving seasoned wood, your piece may look more finished. When carving greenwood, don't worry if it looks "shaggy" or rougher. Get your piece to the right shape, then let it dry and finish it later with cleaner cuts.

> **DO IT BETTER**
>
> If wood dries too quickly, it may split or crack (called "checking"). To avoid this, store it in a cool place, even pack it in wood shavings, and it will dry evenly.

MISSION: Cloud Trees

Spend a lazy afternoon lounging among the trees. Look at the different shapes of branches, limbs, and stumps. Think of them like clouds—imagine what Truly Helpful tool you could craft each one into. Could that straight stick become an arrow shaft? Does that branch have a spoon inside it? Is that limb a future bow?

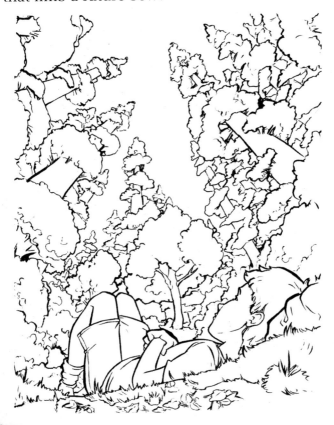

5

The best knife is the knife you got.
—Cowboy Sam

Your Knife

A knife can become a Ranger's most useful tool. The right knife can carve, butcher, and even split wood, meeting almost any need in Forest Craft.

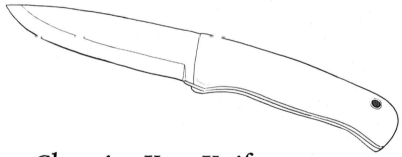

Choosing Your Knife

No perfect knife exists for every situation. Instead, a Ranger makes the best of the tools and materials she has on hand.

Fixed vs Folding

Rangers prefer fixed blades that don't fold. The single steel piece of a fixed blade adds strength and leverage. The moving parts of a folding blade add weak points. Local customs often make it more acceptable to carry a folding blade. If you do carry a "folder", make sure it has a locking mechanism that prevents the blade from pinching back on your fingers.

Edge

Rangers favor a plain-edged blade. Serrated (toothed) blades are useless or unsafe for carving wood. A blade with an edge on only one side is also safer and more practical for most carving grips than a double-edged blade (see page 105 Sharpening Blades for types of grinds and bevels).

Material

Blades can be made of stone, bone, or steel. The material of your blade determines its use and value. High quality carbon steel sharpens efficiently and also holds an edge. While Mariners may choose quality stainless steel because it won't rust at sea, cheaper, inferior knives are often made from it. A Ranger welcomes caring for his carbon steel blade, keeping it dry and conditioning it regularly.

Shape

Shape affects how you wield your knife. Look for an edge that starts close to the handle. The blade width should feel sturdy, but not too cumbersome for finer work. It's good if the point aligns closely to the centerline of the entire knife.

Handle

The handle of your knife should fit comfortably in your hand and allow for a solid grip. Test it out. A rounded handle prevents blisters better than a circle or square. A hand guard can interfere with many knife grips and cuts, while not really improving safety. Make sure the handle is attached securely to the blade.

Size

A simple Forest Craft blade equals a useful blade. With thoughtful carving and proper choice of materials, a smaller knife can do as well or better than a big one. Remember, a Ranger doesn't need a giant blade to hack or cut—or to prove her worthiness. A blade that is 7 to 18 cm long is small enough for fine carving and large enough for heavier tasks. Your comfort and personal Forest Craft style will determine the size of your knife. Local rules might call for a certain length blade. Do your research.

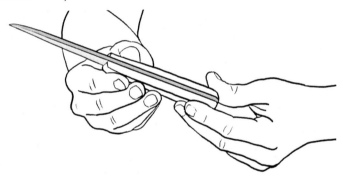

DO IT BETTER

The *tang* of a knife extends the steel of the blade into the handle. A *full tang* runs through the entire handle, while a *partial tang* only runs partway through it. A *slab tang* runs through the width of the handle, visibly sandwiched between two halves. While not required, combined full tang/slab tang makes for a sturdier blade.

Sheathing and Unsheathing

One the most frequent carving injuries occurs when beginners take their blade out of its cover (unsheathing) or put it back in (sheathing). Follow these steps to stay safe:

1. Always hold the sheath near the end, not at the top where the blade comes out. Keep your sheath hand away from the top of the sheath where the knife exits.
2. Use your fingertips to pinch the flat part of the sheath. Don't wrap your hand around the edge of the sheath. This anticipates any flaws in a sheath where the knife could cut through.
3. When unsheathing, put the thumb of your knife hand on the top lip of the sheath and press gently to help unstick your knife as you pull it out.

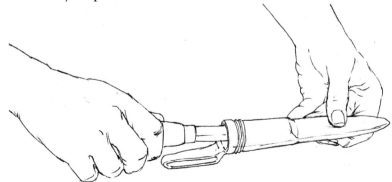

Knife Hand Off

When passing a live knife to a fellow Ranger, offer it handle first and blade edge up. Your thumb and index finger should pinch the top part of the handle.

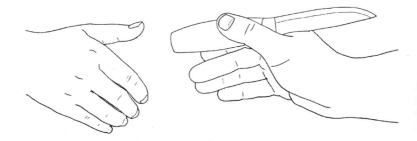

6

*Blades are an extension of your body.
Understand the craft and damage
you're now capable of.*
—Rangers Guild Lore

Carving Stances

Carving stances form the foundations for guarding your Outer and Inner Blood Circles.

Standing

Stand with your feet shoulder-width apart. Loosely bend your knees and sink slightly at the hips. Extend your hands and arms out to keep the carving action away from your Inner Blood Circle.

Kneeling Tall

This stance is also shoulder-width apart, but you stand on your knees instead of your feet. Because your body stands vertical from the knees up, this also keeps the carving action off of your lap.

> **NO ONE DIES**
> Resist the temptation to rest back on your heels or sit down and carve on your lap. In this position, if your blade slips you risk cutting a major artery in your leg (which could kill you and break Rule #1).

Twisting

If you must sit down while carving, you can twist your torso to the side. This takes the carving action away from your lap and out of your Inner Blood Circle.

MODIFY: The Block

You can use a solid surface, like a log round or a table, to help stabilize the wood you're carving. As always, keep everything out beyond your knees and away from the inner thigh.

Sitting

You can sit and carve, so long as you Pay Attention and keep the carving action out of your lap. We ask beginners to twist while sitting since they lack experience, but proper extension or mastery of more advanced cuts changes this.

DO IT BETTER

As you learn from more mentors, you'll see different carving techniques. These are not necessarily wrong. They may be more advanced than the basic stances in this book, or just a different style. As your technique improves, your stances can become more flexible. Watch and think for yourself; understand how you can safely and functionally apply new techniques.

7

Kids (and adults) today don't know how to make a fist. So they can't hold a tool. No wonder the world's about to burn.
—Ranger Chris

Carving Grips

How you hold your knife not only keeps you safe, but can also give you better control and force. Start with the basic grips.

Fist Grip

This grip is used for more powerful cuts and removing lots of wood. Hold the knife handle with a fist in one hand and the wood with a fist in the other. The blade should face away from you. Wrapping the thumb over the top part of the fingers reduces wrist motion, helping you to use the larger muscles of your shoulders and body.

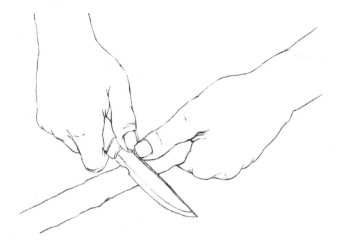

Double-Thumb Grip

For finer, more detailed carving, place both thumbs on the back of the knife to push it forward. This makes shorter cuts, but can be safer and more controlled.

MODIFY

A modify of the Double-Thumb Grip is to put the thumb of the wood hand (hand holding the wood) on top of the thumb of the knife hand (hand holding the knife)—adding another source of power and control.

Backhand Grip

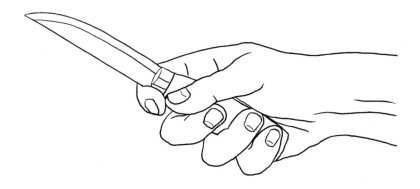

Start with the Fist Grip and rotate the knife so the blade edge faces towards you. Tilt the handle so you're holding it diagonally. For safety, angle the knifepoint away from you at a 15° angle. The Backhand Grip is for intermediate and advanced cuts like the Paring Cut and Pull Cut.

NO ONE DIES

When using the Backhand Grip make sure the tip of the knife always points away from you. Not only does this prevent accidental self-stabbings, it also angles the knife hand to create a "guard," so that the first place of contact with your body would be your hand or the butt of the knife.

MODIFY: Choke-Up Grip

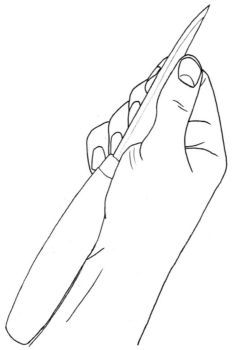

A modify of the Backhand Grip entails choking-up onto the back of the blade. This change-up adds leverage or allows you to use upper parts of the blade. Take great care not to let your knife fingers wrap around any blade edge.

Finger-Reinforced Grip

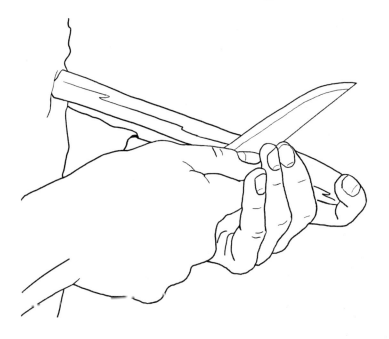

Like the Double-Thumb Grip, this grip uses the fingers of the wood hand to help control and lever the blade. You most often use the Finger Reinforced Grip in advanced cuts. Starting with the Backhand Grip, use the fingers of the wood hand to help push the back of blade.

DO IT BETTER

Like in carving stances, these basic grips are starting points for wielding your knife well. As you gain experience, you won't have to limit yourself to these exact descriptions. When experimenting with new grips, guard your Inner and Outer Blood circles, making certain every possible path of the blade remains clear and safe.

MISSION: Knife-Fu

1. Learn these knife grips and demonstrate them to a fellow Ranger or elder, explaining their particular safety precautions.

2. Teach the knife grips to another Ranger-in-training.

8

Let the growing do the cutting for you.
—Rangers Guild Lore

Carving Secrets

Understanding a few key concepts about carving wood can make your work safer and more efficient.

Angle of Cut

The angle of a cut determines how much wood you take off. Biting deeper into the wood slices off more layers, but often requires more force. Holding the blade flatter against the wood shaves off thinner, finer slices.

Clean Cut

Whatever your angle, keep consistent and firm pressure down on the wood with your knife. This creates cleaner cuts.

Small Cuts Make Bigger Cuts

You can make many smaller and thinner cuts, which build into a larger cut. This is safer and more efficient.

Law of Corners

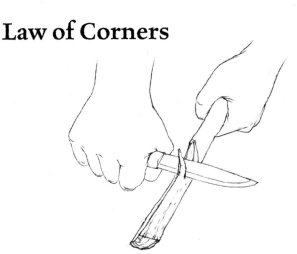

As you carve, a flat spot forms. The wider this flat spot gets, the more wood you have to slice through. New corners form on either side of a flat spot. Carving at these corners can be more efficient.

Move Yourself

When first learning to carve, beginners often twist their arm to turn the wood, which is awkward and unsafe. Instead, be willing to shift positions, rotating the wood in your hands.

Don't Cut the Cheese!

When you cut cheese, you cut with just one part of the blade. Wood is not cheese. When you cut wood, try to use the full blade edge, from the base to the tip or the tip to the base. This prevents dulling on one part of the edge.

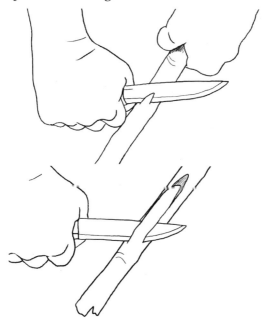

Flip Switch

If you slice too deep through the wood you risk splitting away a larger piece than you intended. If you do cut too deep, flip the piece around and start the cut again from the other side.

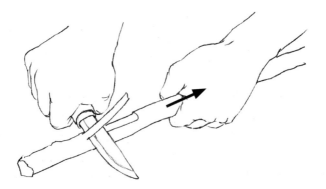

Move The Wood

In many cuts you gain more control and force when you pull or move the wood while pushing forward or simply resisting with your knife.

Change-Up

The willingness to move also applies to what grips and cuts you use. If a particular cut becomes awkward and unsafe, Pay Attention to your piece and consider shifting to a more appropriate grip, cut, or even stance.

Rock The Knife

On occasion, it helps to rock the knife gently into the wood instead of slicing or pushing through. While rocking, the blade moves through the wood in a very slow, controlled manner.

9

A new sailor cautiously cuts away from herself. A seasoned sailor thoughtfully carves towards herself, swearing to the sea gods she never gets a nick. The salty old sea dog goes back to carving away from herself, understanding the first to be a novice, the latter to be a liar.
—Mad Mariner Maude

Basic Cuts

For cuts, we begin with the basics. Remember to always follow the 8 Blades while working with your knife.

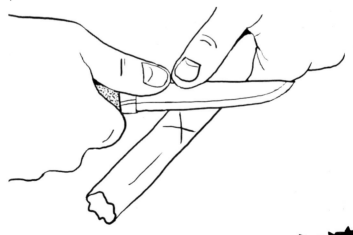

Forward Cut

Most people think of the Forward Cut, the most basic cut, when they think of carving.

1. Hold your knife with a Fist Grip in one hand. Hold the wood with a Fist Grip in your other hand.

2. Position the blade edge onto the wood where you want to start your cut. Don't form a perfect cross with the blade on the wood, instead angle the butt of the handle slightly away from you.

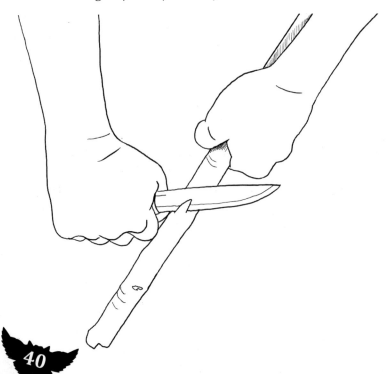

3. Slice forward, away from the wood hand and the rest of your body.

Remember to use the full edge of your blade (don't cut the cheese!). Also, a deeper angle takes off more layers of grain but requires more force. A shallower angle removes thinner slices and can build into bigger cuts.

Practice holding the wood with a Fist Grip by wrapping your thumb over the top part of your fingers. Also, don't tilt your wood hand knuckles. Keep them at right angles to the wood.

NO THUMB DIES

Beginners often make the serious mistake of extending their thumb or fingers to brace the wood while holding it. This frequently leads to people carving off the tips of their digits.

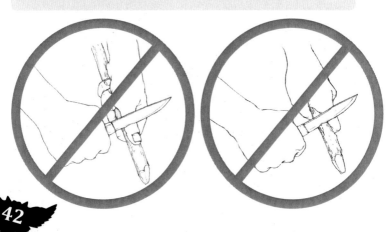

MODIFY: Extension Cut

Use the Extension Cut to better remove bulk amounts of material while shaping wood. It's just like the Forward Cut, but you hold your arms out straight in front of you (no T-Rex arms!). Full-arm extension means you use the larger muscles of your upper body instead of the weaker muscles of your elbow or wrist.

Push Cut

The Push Cut uses the Double-Thumb Grip for more controlled and detailed cuts.

1. Use the Double-Thumb Grip by placing both the wood thumb and knife thumb on the back of the blade.//
2. Position the blade edge onto the wood where you want to start your cut.

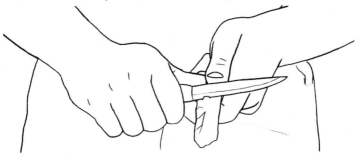

3. Keeping the wood thumb on the back of the blade, push or pivot the knife forward. The knife thumb naturally stabilizes the blade.

The most efficient and effective way to use the Push Cut involves also pivoting the blade on the wood thumb to cut along the length of the knife edge (see page 37 Don't Cut the Cheese).

Remember, you can modify the Double-Thumb Grip by putting the wood thumb on top of the knife thumb.

Stop Cut

Stop Cuts are used to create notches for trap triggers or catches for tent stakes.

1. Using a Double Thumb Grip or placing the wood on a block, press the blade edge straight down into the wood (perpendicular).

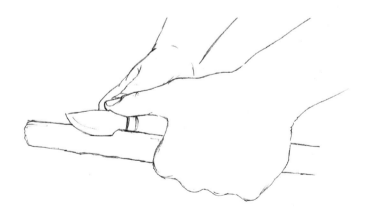

2. Apply downward pressure with the knife and upward pressure with the wood. It helps to slowly rock the knife or wood from side to side.

3. Use the Push Cut to slice towards the Stop Cut. Your slice falls off when your knife reaches the Stop Cut, creating a notch.

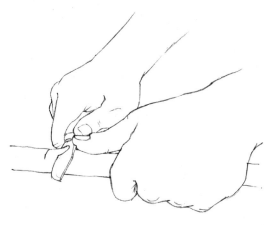

4. If you want to deepen your notch repeat these steps.

NO ONE DIES

Imagine the Stop Cut pushing all the way through the wood. Use that as a guide to position your wood fingers and knuckles well out of the path of the blade. Instead of holding the wood, a safer method for beginners is to use a wood block on a solid surface. Lay your wood on the block, bracing with your wood hand well away from the blade, then apply downward pressure for the Stop Cut.

MODIFY: Cat Notch

This notch looks like the face of a cat and can be used as a hook to hang things from.

1. Make two Stop Cuts in the form an X.

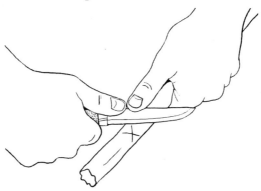

2. With Push Cuts carve through the bottom three quarters of the X so that only the top quarter remains.

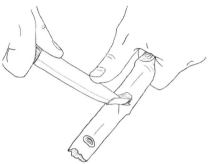

MODIFY: Angled Stop

For Stop Cuts that angle in, like when you're cutting v-notches (grooves), you can use a block as a "third hand". This is necessary when you are working near the end of a piece and can't flip the wood to properly hold the other side. Brace one end of the wood on the block and elevate your wood hand to change the angle of a cut, keeping your wood hand out of the path of the blade. Keep the cutting action close to the block or you risk your knife breaking through thin wood.

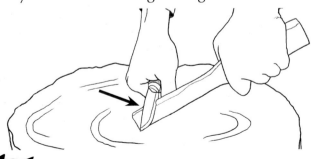

Beaver Chew

Use the Beaver Chew to section a branch (turn one piece into two) without a saw.

1. Cut a ring of flaps around the wood where you want to section it. For thicker wood use the Extension Cut, for thinner sticks use the Push Cut.

2. Flip the branch around and carve another ring of flaps that connects to the first ring. This forms a "valley" all the way around the wood.

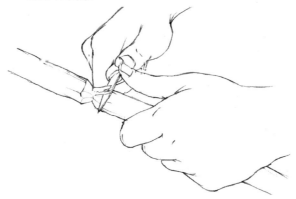

3. Repeat these steps on either side until the "valley" is deep enough that the branch easily snaps in two.

For a cleaner break, continue beaver chewing until the branch falls in two on its own.

Four Directions Cut

To carve a perfect point, think of the directions on a compass.

1. Angle deep into the wood where you want the base of your point to be, and take off one big slice. Rotate the branch a quarter-turn in your hand and cut another slice. Continue rotating and cutting all the way around the Cardinal Directions of the compass: North, East, South, and West.

2. Go around again, but now slice off the Wind Direction corners: Northeast, Southeast, Southwest, and Northwest.

3. Continue to cut each new corner until you have made your point (ha-ha).

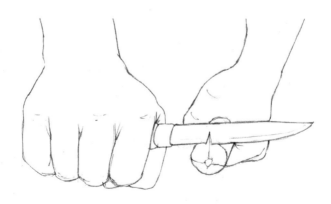

10

Basic Wood Carving Makes

Always be carving. Consistent carving improves more than your woodworking skills; it becomes a meditation, adding to your focus as a Ranger. For these projects you'll need to understand all the Basic Cuts.

Camp Stakes

Rangers use stakes for all kinds of Forest Craft. Small stakes can help secure ropes or brace poles. Big stakes can frame shelter walls.

1. Harvest a knot-free, straight, strong stick about the length of your arm.
2. Use the Beaver Chew to split the stick in two.
3. Use the Four Directions Cut to sharpen the bottom ends of both stakes.

4. Use Forward Cut and Push Cut to slightly round the top ends of the stakes. You can also round the tops by abrading them on a stone. A rounded top prevents the stake from splitting when you hammer it into the ground.

5. Use a Stop Cut and Push Cut to notch each stake near the top to hold rope.

MODIFY: Bullet Point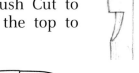

For sturdier points on your stakes, round them into a stouter bullet shape (*ogive*).

MODIFY: Cat Notch

Use a Cat Notch in place of a regular notch to better secure cordage from different angles. (See page 47 for directions)

> ### DO IT BETTER
> Removing bark prevents moisture from collecting around your wood and can increase the durability of what you make.

Willow Whistle

Commonly made from willow, you can carve a whistle from any non-toxic tree with bark that slips off easily. It's easiest to do in the spring because in other seasons it can be difficult to get the bark off.

1. Find a live green shoot of willow, straight and free of knots, so the bark will slip off easily. It should be about as big around as your pointer finger (1-cm thick will do). Later you can experiment with different sizes.

2. Harvest from brushy willow, cutting close to the base of the shrub or main stem so more shoots grow back to take its place (called coppicing).

3. Section with a Beaver Chew or Extension Cut to a length as long or longer than your hand. A longer shoot is easier and safer to hold while you're carving.

4. Use the Extension Cut to make a diagonal cut on one end for the mouthpiece.

5. Cut a small piece off the end, dulling the sharp tip. 1 cm from the mouthpiece, on the long side of the shoot, cut a v-notch across the shoot. Don't make it too deep.

6. About a finger-length down the shoot, score a ring through the bark to the inner wood. Too far down and the bark is difficult to remove, too far up and your air chamber won't be big enough.

7. Tap the bark gently with another stick to loosen it. Don't tap so hard that you damage the bark.

8. Gently twist the bark to loosen it more until it slips off completely. It may require some force, but don't crush it. This bark tube needs to stay intact for your whistle to work.

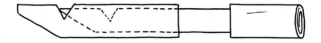

9. Deepen the v-notch to half of the depth of the shoot. A little bit before the end of the bare wood (1 cm), do a Stop Cut to the same depth. Carve from the Stop Cut to the V-notch, making a smooth, flat area between them.

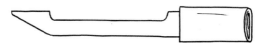

9. Finally, shave off a thin, flat slice of wood from your v-notch to the end of the mouthpiece. This creates an air tunnel. Start thin and adjust later if needed.

10. Slip the bark back into position (it should be a tight fit) and your whistle is done. To play it, just blow.

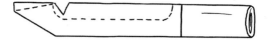

Tune and improve your whistle by increasing the size of the air tunnel or air chamber.

MODIFY: Wilders Willow

When harvesting willow in the spring, take any extra cuttings and stick them in the ground. They may take root, creating more willows for future whistles.

NO ONE DIES

Be sure you know what plant you're harvesting. DO NOT make whistles out of poisonous plants. For example, the bark of the cascara tree is a powerful laxative (which could make you poop most aggressively).

11

Bored? The squirrel and coyote always have a survival project to work on. What makes you so special?
—Wilder Jess

Intermediate Cuts

Intermediate cuts require a deeper understanding of the 8 Blades. Before you attempt any of these, you should practice the Basic Cuts every day for one moon (28 days).

Tree Bending: Felling Saplings and Shoots

With just your knife you can easily fell a sapling or woody shoot thinner than your wrist.

1. Hold the knife with a Fist Grip while bending the tree away from you with your wood hand. Stretching these wood fibers helps the knife slice through more easily.

2. Rocking the knife back and forth, cut at a deep angle where the tree is under the most tension. Your ideal angle is 45°. Since the tree is likely bent at 45° angle, this may "add up" to you cutting straight down (yay, geometry!). Keep applying tension to prevent the knife from binding in the wood.

3. Continue rocking and cutting until the knife makes a clean cut all the way through.

4. Just before you think the trunk is about to "snap," lessen the tension, holding the tree as you finish cutting it, so it doesn't fall (which would cause a jagged break).

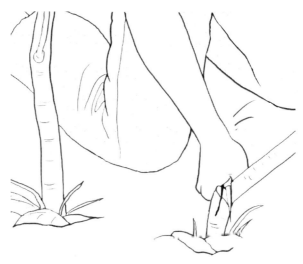

With larger saplings you may need to bend and cut on multiple sides. It helps to have a teammate assist you.

NO ONE DIES
Only harvest saplings that you can easily lift and carry so they aren't a danger when they fall. Saplings can be flexible, so make sure yours doesn't snap back into your face or other breakable parts of your body.

RESPECT

Remember the Southwest Blade: harvest thoughtfully. Consider *coppicing*, which means cutting back certain trees or shrubs to encourage denser growth of new stems. This caretaking practice creates brushier habitat for animals and also more materials for future harvests.

Cutting Limbs

When removing smaller limbs, cut in the direction the branch is growing.

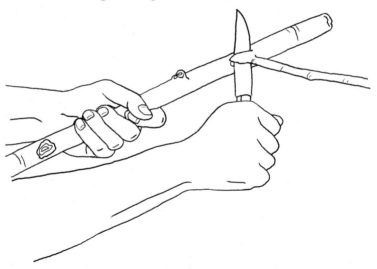

Bopping With a Knife

You can use a sturdy knife to split and shape small pieces of wood.

1. Using the Fist Grip, hold the knife-edge straight against a stable piece of wood where you want to cut or split it. Make sure the tip of the knife extends beyond the wood.

2. With a stout piece of wood, gently tap the back of the blade until it sticks into the wood.

3. Repeatedly hit the point of the knife, working your way down into the wood until a piece falls away.
4. If your knife gets stuck, jerking the blade out is an easy way to get injured. Instead, gently rock it out. If that doesn't work, use a wood wedge (see page 55).

Unlike other cuts, with bopping it may feel more comfortable to bop with your dominant hand and brace the knife in your non-dominant hand.

DO IT BETTER
Bopping can break weaker or poorly made knives, especially if you hit a knot. A knife with a full tang holds up better. Using wedges is the preferred method for splitting (see page 65), as it's the best way to protect your knife.

MODIFY: Bopping Limbs & Knots

Use bopping to remove limbs and knots from a sapling or large branch:

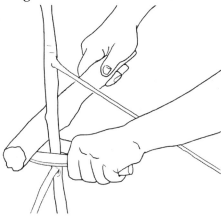

1. Cut in the direction the branch is growing, and keep the blade flush (flat against) with the main stem. Keep the wood stable and secure.
2. Bop the limbs or knots off the main branch.
3. If the sapling or branch lies horizontally on the ground, stand out of the way of the cut.

MODIFY: Bopping to Split Wood

You can split small diameter firewood with bopping. To avoid nicking your knife, don't bop it all the way through into the ground, or use a stable wood block for chopping.

MODIFY: Bulk Removal Bopping

You can use bopping for bulk removal of wood. Since bopping requires you to use both hands, one for the knife and one to bop, the wood must be secured vertically and firmly. One good method is to wedge the top part of your wood into a tree or other secure point, and the bottom into the ground or a root, so it does not slip forward. Then you can have both hands free to bop wood off the sides of your piece.

MODIFY: Bopping with Wedges

Using wedges can free a stuck knife and can also make bopping more efficient. Remember, the wood wedge is your friend.

1. Find or carve a wedge of wood. The top part should be thicker than the blade of the knife, and a bottom part should be thin enough to wedge into the split where your blade is stuck.

2. Bop the wedge into any part of the split, straight into the top or along the side.

3. For easier and more controlled splitting, use several wedges all the way along the side and on both sides of the wood until it splits.

Chest Lever Cut

The Chest Lever Cut gives you more force by using the stronger muscles of your chest and back. When performed properly it also offers more control. Even though this cut occurs near your body, it can be done safely because you limit movement by bracing your arms against your chest.

1. Hold your knife in a Backhand Grip. Turn both your knife and wood hands so you look down on your fingernails. The blade edge should face away from you.

2. Brace your hands halfway up your torso, near your rib cage. The knifepoint should be angled about 45° away from your chest, with the blade edge facing out. The knife and wood should form an X.

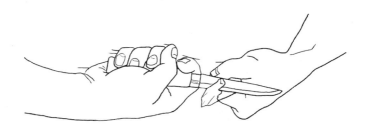

3. Pull both arms apart in a short motion, cutting away from yourself and through the wood. While cutting, keep your hands pressed against your ribcage, which uses the stronger muscles of your chest and back and safely limits any wide slicing movements.

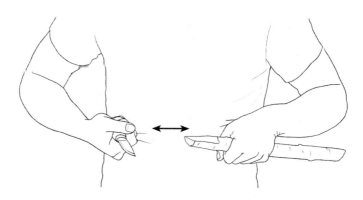

Remember, Don't Cut the Cheese, start your slice at the base of the blade and run to the tip. The Chest Lever Cut may feel strange at first, but it becomes a useful change-up to many basic cuts and should get more comfortable each time you use it.

NO ONE DIES

When doing the Chest Lever Cut, don't carve upward. You don't want to stab yourself in the face.

MODIFY: Knuckle Edge Grip

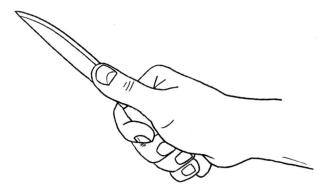

The Knuckle Edge Grip is the preferred method for the Chest Lever Cut, but can feel awkward for beginners. Instead of using the full Backhand Grip, turn the blade edge so it faces your big knuckles (still only holding the handle), and rest your knife thumb on the flat of the blade.

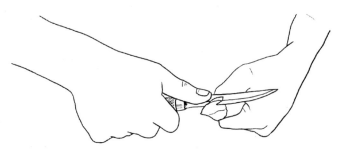

Square Holes

Square holes take advantage of your knife's ability to severe and lift away the wood fibers.

1. Flatten the wood where you want to put your hole, so you don't need to cut through too many layers.

2. Using a modified Stop Cut, press the knifepoint in to score four sides of a small square. Don't start too wide—lifting out the wood fibers becomes difficult.

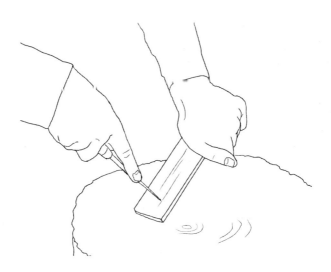

3. Use the knifepoint to lift the wood fibers out of the scored area. Take care to not pry so hard that you break the knife tip (easy to do with hard or seasoned wood). Instead, pull up just a few thin layers, then rescore to add depth each time.

4. When your hole goes halfway through the wood, draw or score light lines marking the top and bottom of the hole and run those around to the opposite side. Use them as guides to begin carving out the other half of your hole.

5. Repeat steps 1-3 on the other side until they both meet to make a hole through the wood.

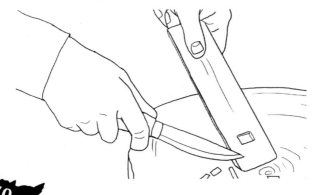

NO ONE DIES

When scoring the small sides of the square or lifting away fibers, resist the temptation to cradle the wood in the palm of your hand or set it on any part of your body (such as your leg). Instead, place it on a woodblock and keep your wood hand as far from the knifepoint as possible. Raise the wood hand up with the hole end on the block. This prevents the knife from slipping along the wood and into your hand.

MODIFY: Rectangles

Rectangles running with the grain are as simple to create as squares. When you want to carve a wider hole, it's more efficient to create several thin rectangles side by side.

1. Stand the blade perpendicular to the wood. Using a modified Double Thumb Grip, place the wood thumb behind the knife tip. Push the knifepoint along the wood grain to make two long parallel scores.

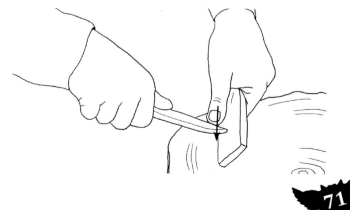

2. Score the shorter sides, forming a rectangle, and lift out the wood fibers the same way you would a smaller square.

As the knifepoint travels forward, the wood hand pushing the tip should also inch along but keep out of the path of the blade. If the knife punctures the wood, this keeps you from stabbing your wood hand.

Knife Engraving

While right angles (squares and rectangles) take advantage of the structure of the wood grain, you can carve v-shaped grooves to engrave lines for letters, patterns, and shapes into the wood.

1. With the knifepoint, use the same modified Double Thumb Grip or Stop Cut from Square Holes to score at an angle. The angle depends on how deep you want your engraving line.

2. Score another line parallel to the original (also at an angle)—cutting out a thin v-shaped groove.

3. The narrower the space between your lines, the steeper your groove. You can use different angles with your cuts to make different shapes. You can also use very shallow angles to cut out "chips".

Curved lines can be challenging at first. Make sure your have full control of your blade while scoring. Such fine work is usually easier with shorter knife blades.

NO ONE DIES

Scoring the wood at an angle risks the knifepoint skipping out of the wood and slipping into your wood hand. The more shallow the angle the higher the risk. As always, Pay Attention and make sure your thumb and fingers remain out of any potential path of the blade.

12

Intermediate Wood Carving Makes

For these carving projects, you will need to know how to do all the Intermediate Cuts.

Digger-Bopper

The Digger-Bopper can work as a bopping tool for your knife, a digging stick for harvesting roots and building shelters, and a throwing stick for hunting small game. It's the Ranger's multi-tool.

1. Start with a branch of straight grain and sturdy wood that is thicker than your thumb, but thinner than your wrist.

2. Use Bopping or Forward Cut to Beaver Chew a section that measures from your armpit to the tips of your fingers.

3. Use Bopping to rough one end into a point for digging. Use Extension Cut and Push Cut to further shape the point. As with stakes, you can make it sturdier by carving an ogive shape.

4. Round the edges of the other end, leaving the top fairly flat. You'll want it flat because when you dig with it, you will brace it with one hand on top and the other hand holding the middle.

To throw a Digger-Bopper (for hunting or target practice), you release it off your top-three fingers in a whip-like motion. To practice your throwing power and accuracy, you can set up a Digger-Bopper "range" using standing log rounds and sticks for targets (stand-ins for rabbits and squirrels—mmmm, dinner).

NO ONE DIES
For safety, make sure there is nothing and no one behind your Digger-Bopper range, and that no one walks through it while you're practicing. It does not feel good to get hit with a Digger-Bopper.

Memdrum

A Memdrum is a flat slat of wood carved into a wing shape. It's tied to the end of a cord and spun rapidly to make an eerie, vibrating sound.

1. Bop a thin flat of wood from a thick branch—about 5 cm wide by 20 cm long by 1 cm thick. It can be almost any size, but has to be heavy enough to gain momentum while spinning and light enough to spin rapidly.
2. Carve ogive points on both ends.
3. Carve a blade-like edge all the way around the piece. The edge should round smoothly into the flatter areas.
4. Cut a square hole on one end, large enough to thread your string through.

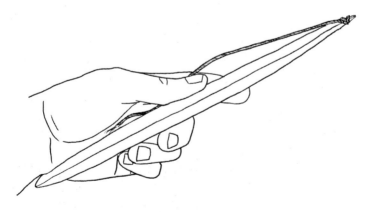

5. Tie a secure knot with enough extra string to allow full swings—about 1-2 meters will do.

To use the Memdrum, first *twist* the string—this gets it whirling while you spin it. If you spin it horizontally above your head, let out more string. If you spin it vertically to the side, use less string. If it's not making a sound, twist the string more before you swing it.

MODIFY: Memdrum Tuning

Experiment with different shapes, lengths of string, and rates of spin, to make different sounds.

NO ONE DIES

Follow the Code of Common Sense. Your Memdrum has its own Outer and Inner Blood Circles. Careless swinging can cause you to smack yourself or someone else. You should also make sure your knot is secure and won't slip.

13

"Advanced" can mean two things: you've practiced diligently and know you're ready; or you're really curious, hurt yourself, and learned an "advanced" lesson. Unless you're dead, then that's awkward.
—Old Man Jacobson

Advanced Cuts

Many advanced cuts involve carving toward yourself, but utilize various stops for safety. *Do not* practice any advanced cuts until you're experienced enough to fully control your blade. Practice Intermediate Cuts every day for one moon (28 days) before moving on to Advanced Cuts. Even this is not a perfect measure—you must develop your own judgment about when you're ready.

With all Advanced Cuts, first practice very small strokes until you can fully control the knife.

Pull Cut

When you want to carve away from the end of a piece of wood, you often don't have a secure place to hold it. With the Pull Cut, you can work this area safely, from the end of the wood down its length.

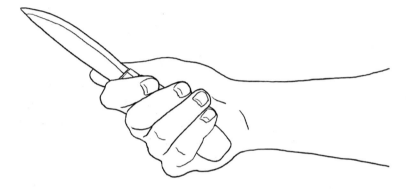

1. Use a modified Backhand Grip. Place your thumb on the same side of the blade as your bottom knuckles. The outer side of your thumb should press diagonally across the flat of the blade, which provides more bracing power and control.

2. Brace one end of the wood comfortably against your chest while holding the other end with your wood hand. All carving takes place between the wood hand and your chest.

3. Press your elbows or forearms firmly against your sides, and pull your knife wrist close to the wood. Both these actions help stop the blade from hitting you.

4. As a final safety stop, your knifepoint should always angle away from you to make sure your knife hand or the butt of the handle hits your chest before the edge ever can.

5. Pull the knife towards your chest, making fine shavings down the wood. Remember to keep your arms pressed against your sides so the blade can't slip and cut your chest (T-Rex arms, woo-hoo).

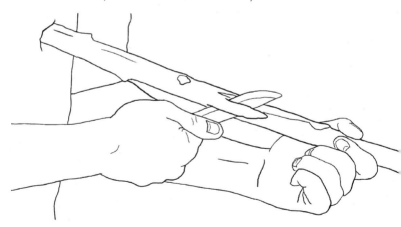

Remember the key safety features: tip of the knife points away from you, arms tight to your sides, wrists pulled in toward wood.

> ### DO IT BETTER
> Always do a full edge slice (Don't Cut the Cheese!). Also, it can be easier to move the wood along the edge of the blade.

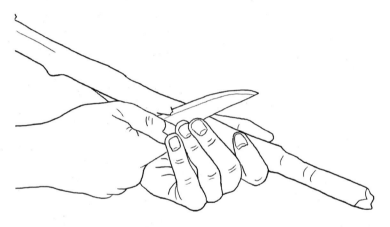

MODIFY: Finger Reinforced Grip
Modify the Pull Cut with the Finger Reinforced Grip to do intricate cuts around difficult areas. Holding the wood with your thumb and index finger, place all or some of your wood hand fingers on the back of the blade. The hold varies with the size of the wood and the path of your cut.

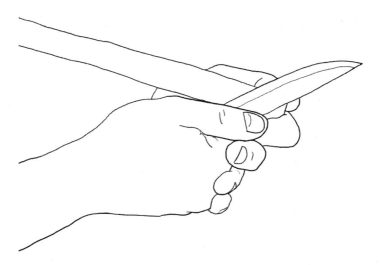

MODIFY: Cupping

When you need greater agility for very tight areas, and when you are choking up on the blade, you can modify your hold so your wood hand cups your knife hand to help guide it. Another modify is to place the knuckles of the knife hand against the knuckles of the wood hand.

NO ONE DIES

Make sure the wrist of your wood hand always remains out of any potential path of the blade, especially when working thin pieces using the Finger Reinforced Grip, Cupping, or Knuckle to Knuckle. Imagine if the piece broke, would the blade cut into your wrist? You can arch your wrist outward, keeping it out of the knife's path.

Paring Cut

This cut is good for controlled carving when the wood is difficult to hold for a Forward Cut.

1. Holding the knife in the Backhand Grip, ready to cut toward yourself, place your knife thumb on the end of the wood that is closest to your chest. Keep your thumb out of the way of any potential path the blade can take.

2. Place your wood hand behind the back of the blade so that you're carving between the wood hand and your knife thumb.

3. Draw the knife through the wood, letting the blade edge follow a path to the empty space between the thumb and index finger. Remember to keep the knifepoint angled away from you.

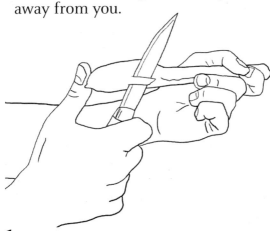

4. Make your cuts across the full edge of your knife. Start at the hilt and slice to the tip of the knife, or vice versa. Moving the wood can help make this cut easier.

NO THUMB DIES

It's *very important* that you keep your knife thumb fully out of the way of the blade. Some people wear a leather thumb guard, but when you perform this cut correctly you always keep your thumb out of the carving path.

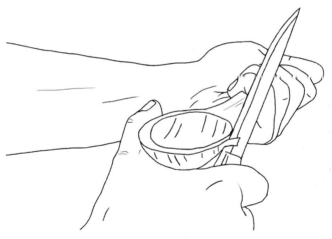

MODIFY: Thumb Grasp Paring

With practice, you can place the knife thumb on another side of the wood (not just the end) to grip the piece while making the cut. This is often the most practical version of the Paring Cut.

Thumb Pivot Cut

Though one of the most technically complex cuts, the Thumb Pivot Cut is quite useful in carving. The cut starts in a similar position to the Paring Cut, but allows you to place the thumb of the knife hand on the same side of the wood you are carving. Pay Attention and make sure you've practiced enough to keep full control of your blade.

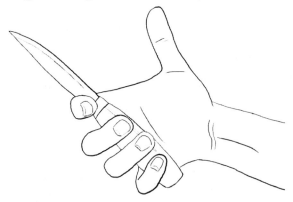

1. Hold the knife in a Backhand Grip, but hold the handle only with your fingers; *do not* let the handle touch your palm.

2. Curl the knuckle of your index finger slightly over the back and flat of the blade, choke up past the hilt and just over the handle, but do not let it touch the blade edge. This creates a safety stop for your cut. You can also put your fingertip on the flat of the blade.

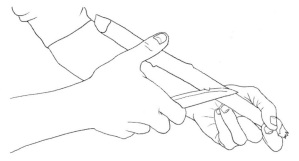

3. Place your knife thumb on the wood, holding it as far from the blade edge as possible.

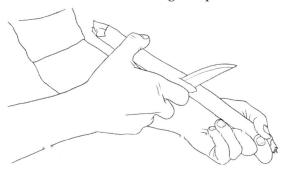

4. Unlike the Paring Cut *do not* open and close your palm. Instead, use the muscles of your lower thumb joint as a pivot point. Rotate the knife hand up to make a cut that starts at the tip and moves down along the edge of the blade.

5. Your knife index finger stops the blade well before the edge reaches the thumb.

Like many cuts, you can rotate the wood, not just your hand, to help with control and power.

NO ONE DIES

Remember to use the stop of your index finger to make only small cuts, and keep your palm fully open to maintain safe distance between your thumb and the blade.

Nock Cut

Use the Nock Cut to *haft* (secure) arrowheads, spears and other tools to a *shaft* (straight stick) or to bind two sticks together.

1. Plan out your nock. Picture a square shaft running inside the length of your stick.

2. First make two "start" v-notches on opposite sides of the stick. Cut them deep enough that they touch that imaginary square shaft inside your stick.

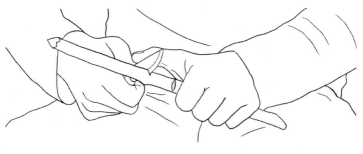

3. Leave room so you can hold the stick above your "start" v-notches. This allows you to flip the stick so you don't need to angle the knife towards your wood hand when making the top part of the v-notch.

4. Make two more "stop" v-notches further down the remaining sides of the imaginary square (90° from your first v-notches). The distance depends on how long you need your nock to be.

5. Beginning at a start v-notch, rock the knife or stick back and forth, slowly working down to the stop v-notch. *Do not slice*, as you risk breaking through the stop v-notches.

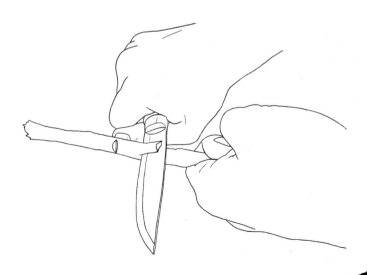

6. Press your knifepoint into both stop v-notches to help the wood break cleanly.

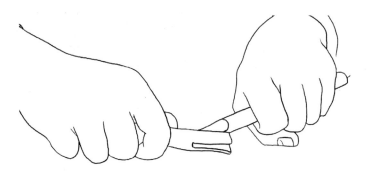

MODIFY: Lever Version
With your thumbs, use gentle pressure at the start v-notches to lever the wood and begin a split down towards the stop v-notches. Apply pressure, slowly making your way down to continue the split. Don't apply so much force that you break through beyond the stop v-notches. Once you reach the stop v-notches, gently break out the nock on both sides.

Different sticks and shoots will split more cleanly than others. To get it right, this cut requires a lot of practice and understanding of materials.

NO ONE DIES

Sometimes experienced people think they're invincible and forget to leave enough room to grasp the stick above the nock. When they slice toward their hand during the splitting stage, they often end up with a bloody mess.

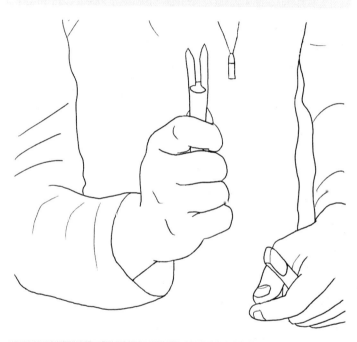

DO IT BETTER

Like stances and grips, as you gain real experience you might modify any basic, intermediate, and advanced cut. You may even mix different cuts together. How you grow as a carver is your responsibility.

14

Advanced Wood Carving Makes

For these projects you'll need to understand and practice all the Advanced Cuts.

Net Needle

This is both a spool and a needle for weaving fishing nets, but it has many other uses. When lashing thatch for shelter or other Forest Craft projects, a net needle helps avoid a tangled mess.

1. Bop a thin flat board out of a sectioned branch. The width and length of the board depend on how much twine you want to hold. 4 cm wide by 8 cm long is a good starting size. Bop and shave this board down to 1/2 cm thick.

2. Carve one end into an ogive shape.

3. Score and lift out two long, parallel rectangle holes starting at the base of the ogive and running 1/3- 1/2 the length of the board.

4. At the ogive end, carve out the wood to connect the rectangles. Round the top to form a "U".

5. Thin, round, and point the "needle" at the center of the U-shape.

6. At the end of the board opposite the ogive, carve a half square and then round the corners.

7. Round out all edges of the piece. Sand and burnish it with a rock to finish your work.

To spool your net needle, start wrapping twine at the center needle, then down around one side of the notch at the bottom, alternating sides with each wrap.

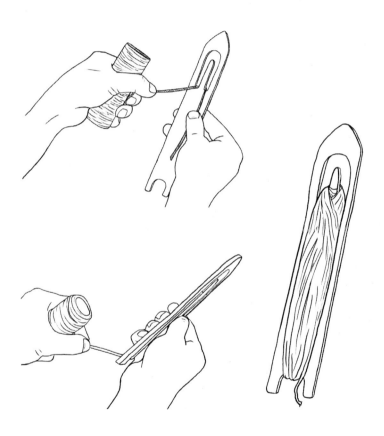

Wood Spoon

Carving a spoon challenges you with all levels of cuts: basic, intermediate and advanced.

1. Use bopping to split a straight-grained branch nearly in half, but leave out the pith (very center of the wood). The length determines the maximum possible length of the spoon and the width determines maximum possible width of the bowl.

2. With charcoal, draw your spoon on the halved wood. This really helps, especially making the bowl of the spoon.

3. Use bopping to remove the largest pieces and Extension Cut to roughly shape it.

4. Use Pull Cut to carve out the "shoulders" of the bowl.

5. Use Forward Cut, Push Cut, Paring Cut, and Chest Lever Cut to round out the bottom of the bowl.

6. As you whittle away the original charcoal lines, redraw them, refining the shape of your spoon.

7. Carving out the bowl of the spoon can be challenging. Woodcarvers often use a specialized knife with a hook-shaped blade. A straight blade still works: you can "trough" by using the techniques outlined in Square Holes and Engraving. Your bowl will be rough, so you'll need to abrade it (see page 104). The better method is to use the Fire Knife (see next Modify).

NO ONE DIES

Remember, when using a straight blade to carve out the bowl, don't cradle the wood in your hand or place it on any part of your body.

MODIFY: Fire Knife

A far superior and safer Forest Craft technique for making the bowl of the spoon does not involve using a blade. You use fire instead.

1. Use tongs to pile still glowing coals from a fire onto the spot where you want to remove wood.

2. Blow on it—hard enough to get the coals burning into the wood, but slow enough so they don't burst into flame. Too much heat will crack the wood, too little and the coals will die out. Be careful not to blow a loose coal onto the ground where it could start a fire.

3. As the coals die down, put them back into the fire and then scrape away the charred area with a rock. Repeat the process until your spoon bowl is as deep as you want it.

When thoughtfully applied, this technique saves a tremendous amount of work. The Fire Knife can also be used to section long lengths of wood into smaller logs, instead of using Beaver Chew.

DO IT BETTER
Pack wet mud along the edges of your bowl to control where your fire goes and the shape that your Fire Knife "cuts".

14

Steel makes you weak. Rock on.
—Ranger Chris

Rock Work

We've covered the relatively recent technology of the metal knife, which can make carving wood more convenient. Rocks, however, will always be one of a Ranger's primary woodcraft tools. Rocks are also very useful in refining or finishing projects you've made using a steel blade.

Scraping

You can use a rock with an edge to scrape away and smooth trouble areas. Bone also works well.

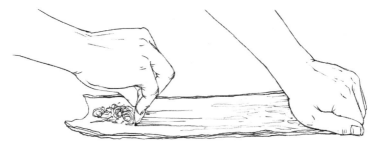

Abrading

You can use coarse stones to sand rough areas of wood, just like sandpaper. A Ranger can look at different rocks and see how their shape and coarseness can be used to abrade wood. Look for this in the stones you collect.

Burnishing

You can use smoother rocks to polish your wood to a glossy surface that helps finish a piece. Rub the rock across the wood while applying firm pressure that compresses and seals the wood fibers.

15

Sharpen your knife, sharpen your life.
—Ranger Jamey

Sharpening Blades

A sharp blade is Truly Helpful. A dull blade struggles and can cause injury. The more attuned you become to your blade, the more you notice slight changes in how it moves through wood, and the quicker you'll know it's time to sharpen.

Bevel and Grind

Look closely at your knife. You'll see an area along the edge of the blade where the metal starts sloping toward the sharp edge. That's called the *bevel*. The *grind* is simply the different shapes of the bevel. To maintain most blades, you usually need to recognize two types of bevels.

Primary Bevel

The primary bevel is the first place the blade angles into an edge. This could start anywhere on the flat of the blade. Sometimes a knife grind has only one bevel, so that the entire thickness of the blade angles into the edge.

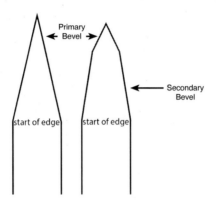

Secondary Bevel

A secondary bevel is when the angle of the primary bevel changes to another bevel. Not all knives have a secondary bevel; you have to look closely to see it.

The bevel that forms the cutting edge determines the angle you sharpen your knife at. Sharpen at the bevel that forms the edge of your blade.

Sharpening Stones

To sharpen your blade, you'll need the right surface. This could be a stone crafted specifically for sharpening, or even a flat rock with the proper *grit* (roughness). You can tell the level of grit by the type of scratches a stone leaves on your blade. Stones made specifically for sharpening are often numbered—the lower the number the coarser or rougher the grit.

Rough Stone (Coarse Grit) *Sharpening with a rough stone leaves visible scratches on your blade.* A rough stone removes the greatest amount of material from the blade and leaves a rougher edge. Only use a rough stone when you have to repair or reshape a nicked or extremely dull blade.

Middle Stone (Medium Grit) *Sharpening with a middle stone leaves light scratches on your blade.* A middle stone removes less material from your blade and leaves a smoother edge. Depending on the sharpness of your blade, you might begin with a middle stone.

Finishing Stone (Fine Grit) *Sharpening with a finishing stone leaves your blade looking frosted to polished.* Use a finishing stone to put a finer edge on a blade and for consistent sharpening.

BE TRULY HELPFUL

Use the grit your blade needs. If you grind too much material off your blade, you shorten its lifespan and its usefulness. Give your blade a lifetime of being Truly Helpful.

MISSION: Rock Rainbow

Build up your collection of sharpening stones.

1. Collect a set of all three grits of stone: coarse, medium, and fine.

2. Then seek out grits that are in between: very fine, very coarse and so on.

3. Pay Attention. Don't just go with what the numbers tell you. Use your senses—eyes, ears, and touch—to "grade" stones yourself. With practice you will get good at judging the usefulness of any stone.

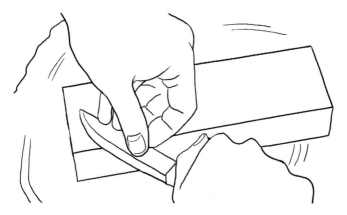

Whetstones vs Water Stones

Whet doesn't mean "wet," but means "to make sharp". To confuse things even more, there are *whetstones* and *water stones*. Water stones must be soaked in water before you use them to sharpen a blade. Whetstones don't have to be soaked first.

For most stones, however, it's a good idea to keep them wet when sharpening. Wetting a stone keeps the *swarf* (bits of metal scraped off the blade) out of the pores. Keeping a stone's pores clean keeps it abrasive.

MODIFY: Sandpaper & Boards

Any abrasive surface can sharpen a knife: sandpaper, emery boards, and more. If you don't have stones, use what you can find. You can gauge the grit by feel and by using the same observations as above.

The Burr

The naked eye cannot fully see the incredible micro-wonderland of sharpening steel. On a very fine level, using coarse grit leaves a sharp but jagged edge. This edge initially cuts well but dulls quickly. As you move up to medium grit, that edge evens out, but the blade still dulls somewhat quickly. A fine grit refines this even more.

Throughout the sharpening process, a tiny strip of metal, called a *burr*, forms on the edge of the knife. You can't see the burr. Carving rips the burr away. The thicker the burr, the duller the edge that's left behind. Each time you move to a finer grit, you create a thinner burr. Use this process, along with the tips below, to reduce the size of the burr and improve your edge.

Unsharpened blade with burrs on the edge (magnified 250X)

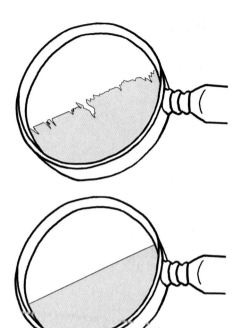

Blade sharpened on finer grit with smoother edge

1. *Do not* drag the blade backward across the stone. Instead, *push it* forward as though removing extremely fine slices from the stone.

2. When you strop on leather or another material (see below), pull back. Moving forward would cut the material. When you thin the burr with finer grits, then stropping removes the last bit evenly. This leaves a stronger, sharper edge behind.

Sharpen Your Knife, Sharpen Your Life

Just like your skills, your blade can always be sharper. Sharpening blades requires thoughtful practice, as well as Paying Attention to your edge.

1. Place the sharpening stone on a flat surface where it will not jostle.
2. Holding the back of the blade, tilt your knife slightly so the bevel is flat against the stone. If your knife has only a Primary Bevel, you can gauge the angle when you feel and hear it *click* onto the stone. If your knife has a Secondary Bevel, you will need to look carefully at your angle when grinding to make sure it's correct.

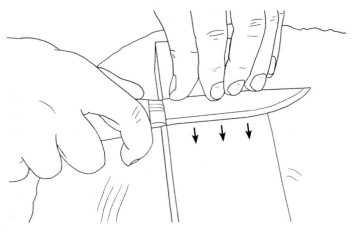

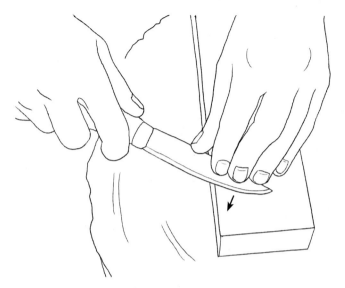

3. Keeping the knife in that angled position along the bevel, move it carefully forward, maintaining pressure as though cutting the very thinnest of slices across the surface of the stone.

4. Sharpen the entire blade. Near the end of the stroke, be sure to follow the curve of the point. You may need to lift the handle to match the bevel angle along a curved point.

5. Always Pay Attention, keeping a consistent angle while sharpening. Don't press too hard. The knife should move easily across the stone while maintaining contact along the bevel.

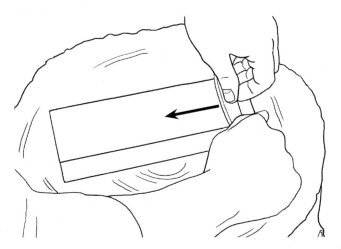

6. To sharpen the other side of the blade, flip it over and pull it towards you on the stone to maintain the motion of thin slicing.

7. Do eight strokes on each side of your blade—one for each of the 8 Blades.

8. Finally, alternate one stroke on each side of the blade for eight more strokes.

9. Each time you move through the 8 Blades, use a cloth to wipe the *swarf* off the blade, taking care not cut yourself.

NO ONE DIES
Blade safety also applies when you are sharpening, especially when you pull the blade towards you. Always maintain control.

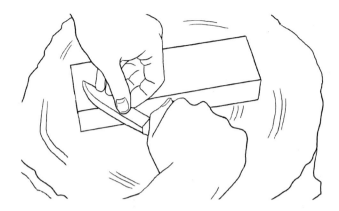

Move up to finer grits, if available, and repeat. For nicks and exceptionally dull spots, you may have to first use a circular motion, grinding on a coarse stone, to reshape that area. If you have a narrower stone in relation to the size of your blade, consider sharpening in sections: first the straight edge and then the point.

DO IT BETTER

The number of strokes varies with the condition of the blade and the grit of the sharpening surface. While we recommend at least 24 strokes for each grit, as you move up to finer grits it helps to double or triple the number of strokes.

Test It

A razor sharp blade carves fine shavings from wood like butter. It will also easily slice a loosely held sheet of paper—if the paper tears, your blade still needs sharpening.

MODIFY: Stropping

Barbers often use a *strop* (leather strip) to keep their razors sharp. You can strop your blade using your own long piece of heavy leather (such as a belt) or even rough fabric.

1. Secure the fabric to something so you can pull it tight with one hand or lay it on a surface where you can easily strop the blade back and forth.

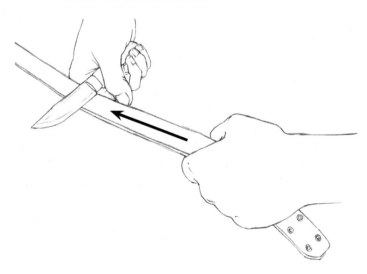

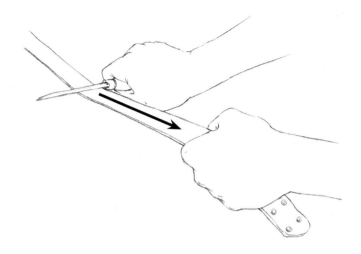

2. Lay the bevel flat to the leather or fabric. Pull the blade opposite a cutting motion, while alternating strokes. Do not pull it blade-edge first or you will cut your strop.

3. Strop after each use of your blade to keep it extra sharp.

Care and Storage

Remember the Northwest Blade: *Practice Blade Discipline.* That means sheath your knife when you're not using it. That's for safety, but it also keeps it free of dirt, moisture, and nicks. Always dry your knife when it gets wet, and oil it periodically to help it stay rust-free.

16

There will be blood.
—Old Man Jacobson

First Aid

Even experienced Rangers accidentally cut themselves from time to time. If you're not ready for that, put this book down now and go enjoy a quiet life.

If you *do* want to work with blades (and I'm guessing you do, since you're almost to the end of the book), be prepared for blood. Here's what to keep in mind.

Don't Panic

Some people see blood and panic. Not helpful. Instead you can calmly *DO* something about the injury.

First Blood
(and Second and Third and So On)

If you never need to practice this skill, you win at being a Ranger (collect your prize at our secret headquarters). But if you *do* get a cut, treat it right away to limit the damage and prevent infection.

1. Make sure there's no risk of further injury from nearby tools or other hazards.

2. Limit the flow of blood by applying direct pressure on the wound. Use a sterile bandage or dressing.

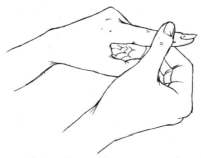

3. Thoroughly clean the wound with water (and soap if you have it) to prevent infection.

4. Apply a sterile dressing to keep the wound clean.

BE TRULY HELPFUL

If a fellow Ranger helps you treat a cut, keep your bodily fluids to yourself by having your teammate wear non-porous, sterile gloves. Did we mention you should keep everything sterile?

When To Seek Serious Medical Care

Many cuts can be treated with basic first aid. Others require more experienced medical treatment. This includes, but is not limited to:

- If the wound won't stop bleeding. If you cut a major artery, it is a very serious emergency. You could die. You need to get proper medical attention as soon as possible.

- If you can see yellow fatty tissue or you can't pinch the wound together. The cut may need stitches.

- If you have trouble moving an appendage (like a finger). You may have cut a tendon.

- If you lose feeling in an appendage or other body part. You might have cut or damaged a nerve.

- If the wound doesn't heal and/or becomes inflamed. It could be infected, which can get very serious very fast. Watch for redness, swelling, loss of function, and/or pain.

- If a finger or other appendage is severed from your body. This needs to be fixed by someone experienced. Your first priority is to stop the bleeding and seek serious medical treatment. Keep the detached part dry and cold, but not frozen.
- If it's a puncture, which can drive pathogens (germs) deep into the flesh.
- If your tetanus vaccination isn't current.
- If it's a Zombie bite.

In any of these instances, immediately seek out more serious medical treatment to prevent permanent injury or even death (both of which would break Trackers Rules #1 and #2).

NO ONE DIES

Fun fact: Tetanus is a horrific, possibly fatal disease. Tetanus bacteria *(Clostridium tetani)* use endospores, survival pods that allow them to live all around us. Once these pods get into the body through a wound, the bacteria invade, causing infection. This infection leads to agonizing muscle spasms and possible death. Be Truly Helpful and get your tetanus vaccination.

Use Common Sense

You can find one million ways to accidentally cut yourself, and many more factors will determine whether you need to seek serious medical attention. This section is *not* comprehensive medical advice. We're Rangers, not doctors, darn it! Like everything in this book, your safety is your responsibility. Cultivate and use your own Common Sense.

MISSION: First Aid Training

Sign up for First Aid training. The knowledge you gain goes beyond simply treating wounds—it makes you Truly Helpful to your family and Village.

MISSION: The Hall of Shame

If and when you get cut, tell the tale to your fellow Rangers. Whenever you tell a story, you relive that experience. Telling how you received a wound helps your friends avoid the same mistake. Prevention and solutions become a part of your Rangers lore. Remember: You're Doing It Wrong, Do It Better. Within the Hall of Shame resides great personal strength. Swallowing your pride, laughing, and celebrating your own imperfections is a powerful Ranger trait. Remember my story at the start of the book about nearly cutting off my thumb? I too am a proud member of the Hall of Shame.

The Rangers Edge

Since the dawn of time there have been Rangers. They live as protectors of the Village: hunters, warriors, and scouts...the shadows living on the edge of the wilderness.

A Ranger can travel anywhere in the wild and not only survive, but *thrive*. They expertly fade their tracks and move silently through the forest, vanishing as ghosts on the land. Ever aware, a Ranger always Pays Attention.

A Ranger's life has an edge like a blade. You must always stay sharp and ready. In Forest Craft, our survival depends on the blades we carry and the skills we practice—treat them all with honor, discipline and Respect.

As a Ranger, you learn to Remember the old ways of the forest. This book starts you down a path— one that carefully walks the Ranger's Edge.

Rangers Words

Beaver Chew: Sectioning a branch or piece of wood by carving around its diameter.

Bevel: The angle leading to the knife's edge.

Blood Circles: Zones you guard whenever using a blade to keep yourself and others safe.

Bopper: A stout piece of wood used to strike the back of your knife in order to move it through the wood.

Brace: To hold and prevent slippage.

Check: A split that occurs when wood dries unevenly.

Coppice: To cut back certain trees or shrubs to encourage growth of new stems.

Digger-Bopper: A bopper with a point and a rounded end that can be used to dig roots or be thrown as a hunting tool.

Forest Craft: The art of a Ranger and the fullest realization of wilderness survival skills.

Grit: The coarseness of a sharpening surface.

Haft: Secure arrowheads, spears and other tools to a shaft.

Knife Hand: Hand holding the knife.

Live Blade: An unsheathed blade.

Make: Using skills to craft a tool, art or other Forest Craft.

Mission: Exploring, researching or harvesting.

Modify: Varying a skill, Mission or Make.

Ogive: A bullet shape.

Sheath: A cover for a blade.

Stropping: Pulling the knife back along a material surface to refine the edge.

Swarf: Tiny bits of metal scraped off the blade during sharpening.

Tang: The steel of the knife blade that extends into the handle.

Village: A Ranger's family, friends, and forest—what they care for and protect.

Wood Grain: Light and dark layers showing yearly growth in wood.

Wood Knots: A mass of hard wood where the grain changes direction.

Wood Hand: Hand holding the wood.

The Four Guilds

*Each of the Four Guilds plays
an essential part in the Village.*

The Rangers Guild survives as the hunters and protectors of the Village. Versed in the arts of Forest Craft, they train in wilderness survival, tracking, and awareness. They are the eyes and ears of the Village, living completely with the land and tending to it, invisible as the Wind.

The Wilders Guild lives as caretakers, restoring the land to what it once was...and beyond. Through Folk Craft and Wisdom they tend to the balance of the Village, guiding the needs of the people into harmony with the rhythms of life in all seasons, rooted in the Earth.

The Mariners Guild fish and tend to the creeks, rivers, and oceans. Mariners chart their course by the stars, currents, and tides. In trade and salty wisdom, they demand Respect for all the life found in the depths of the Waters.

The Artisans Guild opens our eyes to noble purpose and possibilities. They act as our story keepers; travelers bare-of-foot, walking and sleeping under the twilight sky. They ask one and all: Always keep the hearth fire burning, Remember our story.

About Trackers Earth

Trackers Earth offers camps and outdoor programs for all ages. We provide innovative and award-winning education in nature connection and authentic outdoor skills. Founded in 2004, Trackers Earth has gained a reputation for creating legendary camps and outdoor programs. Our labor, profits, tears, and joys exist to create a village of happy and healthy people connected to the Earth.

We are champions of land and village. We are navigators of an epic world that needs to exist. We are a community that celebrates hearth, family, Respect for the land, and a timeless human story.

Explore **TrackersEarth.com**

The Remembering

Of the lessons contained here,
Remember this one:
You are a child born wild and free.

They might tell you differently, and one day
you may follow them.

But it remains.
In the oldest place that seems a dream.
Walking with the deer. The release of an arrow
The warmth of leaves. Fire under stars.
Blood and dirt. Water and life.
The silence of the elk.

Turn the Arrow back around.
Now is the time, for our very survival.

Notes